Little People, BIG DREAMS™
PRINCE

Written by
Maria Isabel Sánchez Vegara

Illustrated by Cachetejack

Frances Lincoln
Children's Books

Little Prince was the son of a piano player and a jazz singer. He was not born with a crown on his head, but he inherited his father's stage name and the most amazing musical talent ever seen in Minneapolis.

At home, Prince wasn't allowed to play his dad's piano, but that didn't stop him from sneaking down and doing it, anyway. Aged seven, he wrote his first song. It was called "Funk Machine," and it made his sister Tyka dance.

When Prince's parents got divorced, his mother married another music lover who took him to see James Brown, the Godfather of Funk. Prince couldn't help jumping on stage to dance with the chorus girls!

School wasn't his thing, but at the Minnesota Dance Theater, he proved to be a bright student. Prince explored movement and self-expression, longing to mix his music with dance.

He was just 19 when he got a chance to go to California and record his first album. Locked in the studio, he did everything: writing, composing, singing, arranging... even playing all 27 instruments!

But it was his second album, "Prince," that made him a superstar. From that day on, everything he did became a success. He made his own rules and then broke them all... just because he could!

Prince loved moving like a cat in high heels—something that, at the time, only women dared to do. He also used falsetto in many of his songs. Singing at his highest pitch, he could feel the sound shaking above his head.

He lived to be on stage, frontlining his band with spectacular guitar fireworks and the funkiest dancers. After a concert for thousands of fans, he would keep playing all night, just for his friends.

During his career, Prince included amazing female
musicians in his bands: drummers, singers, keyboardists,
and guitar players. These women became not just his close
collaborators, but the inspiration for many of his songs.

He also played the lead actor in a movie named after one of his most beautiful songs, *Purple Rain*. The film became a blockbuster, the song a hymn, and its soundtrack is still one of the greatest albums of all time.

For Prince, everything was music... from an actor's laugh to the sound of a window breaking. When he worked on a movie called *Batman*, the director was amazed by the way he mixed sounds together to create the coolest tracks.

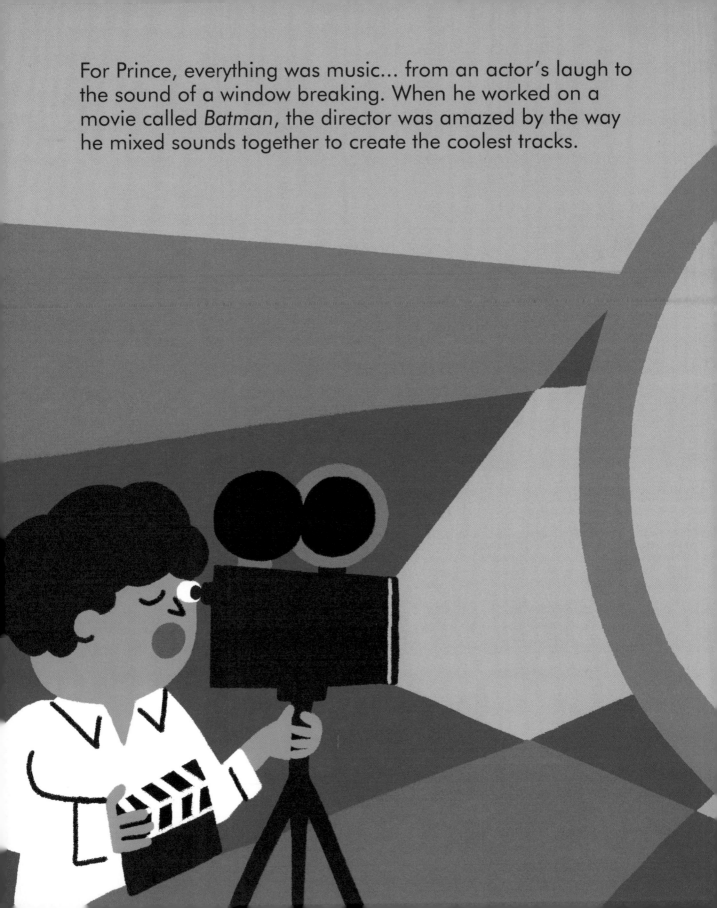

For years, he changed his name to a symbol impossible to pronounce that united the feminine and masculine side in all of us. During that time, people called him "The Artist Formerly Known as Prince:" a free spirit that no one dared to label.

And 1,000 songs later, little Prince—the great mixer of funk, rock, and pop—showed the world that life is not meant to be black or white, but a beautiful rainbow of color... free from limits.

PRINCE

(Born 1958 • Died 2016)

1977

1985

Prince Rogers Nelson was born to two jazz-musician parents in Minneapolis, Minnesota. His parents both had children from previous marriages, and so Prince had eight siblings: one full sister, three half-sisters, and four half-brothers. He was closest to his full sister, Tyka, and spent much of his childhood entertaining her and filling their house with sound. He began playing the piano aged seven and had mastered the guitar and drums by the time he was 14, joining his first band. After his parents divorced, Prince had the life-changing experience of seeing James Brown in concert with his stepfather, Howard Baker. Brown's ability to combine music with movement was inspiring... and so began Prince's quest to bring something original to a world stage. Aged 19, Prince created his first demo, and with the help of

1995

2007

a local Minneapolis businessman, Prince soon had several offers from record companies. His early music began with funk, soul, and disco, moving on later to incorporate a wide influence of sound, including jazz, punk, heavy metal, the Beatles, and hip-hop. Like the many styles of music he experimented with, Prince was not one-dimensional: he also identified as both male and female, celebrating the qualities of both. Today, he is still compared to greats like Stevie Wonder: a rare composer who could perform at a professional level on virtually any instrument he was handed, including his characteristic falsetto voice. Leading by example, Prince's determination to live honestly inspired more than two generations of musicians to experiment and find their own, authentic expression.

Want to find out more about **Prince?**

Have a read of these great books:

40 Inspiring Icons: Black Music Greats by Olivier Cachin and Jérôme Masi

Prince: Singer, songwriter, musician and record producer by David Robson

Brimming with creative inspiration, how-to projects, and useful information to enrich your everyday life, Quarto Knows is a favorite destination for those pursuing their interests and passions. Visit our site and dig deeper with our books into your area of interest: Quarto Creates, Quarto Cooks, Quarto Homes, Quarto Lives, Quarto Drives, Quarto Explores, Quarto Gifts, or Quarto Kids.

First Published in the US in 2021 by Frances Lincoln Children's Books, an imprint of The Quarto Group.
100 Cummings Center, Suite 265D, Beverly, MA 01915, USA.
T +1 978-282-9590 www.QuartoKnows.com

A catalogue record for this book is available from the British Library.
ISBN 978-0-7112-5439-8
Set in Futura BT.

Published by Katie Cotton • Designed by Sasha Moxon
Edited by Katy Flint and Rachel Williams • Production by Nikki Ingram
Manufactured in Guangdong, China CC122020
3 5 7 9 8 6 4 2

Photographic acknowledgements 1. 1977 © Robert Whitman. 2. American singer, songwriter and musician Prince, ca. 1985. © The LIFE Picture Collection via Getty Images. 3. American singer and musician Prince in concert, ca. 1995. © The LIFE Picture Collection via Getty Images. 4. Prince performs during the 'Pepsi Halftime Show' at Super Bowl XLI between the Indianapolis Colts and the Chicago Bears on February 4, 2007 at Dolphin Stadium in Miami Gardens, Florida. © Jonathan Daniel/Getty Images.

Collect the Little People, BIG DREAMS™ series:

FRIDA KAHLO

COCO CHANEL

MAYA ANGELOU

AMELIA EARHART

AGATHA CHRISTIE

MARIE CURIE

ROSA PARKS

AUDREY HEPBURN

EMMELINE PANKHURST

ELLA FITZGERALD

ADA LOVELACE

JANE AUSTEN

GEORGIA O'KEEFFE

HARRIET TUBMAN

ANNE FRANK

MOTHER TERESA

JOSEPHINE BAKER

L. M. MONTGOMERY

JANE GOODALL

SIMONE DE BEAUVOIR

MUHAMMAD ALI

STEPHEN HAWKING

MARIA MONTESSORI

VIVIENNE WESTWOOD

MAHATMA GANDHI

DAVID BOWIE

WILMA RUDOLPH

DOLLY PARTON

BRUCE LEE

RUDOLF NUREYEV

ZAHA HADID

MARY SHELLEY

MARTIN LUTHER KING JR.

DAVID ATTENBOROUGH

ASTRID LINDGREN

EVONNE GOOLAGONG

BOB DYLAN

ALAN TURING

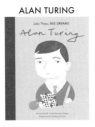

BILLIE JEAN KING

GRETA THUNBERG

JESSE OWENS

JEAN-MICHEL BASQUIAT

ARETHA FRANKLIN

CORAZON AQUINO

PELÉ

ERNEST SHACKLETON

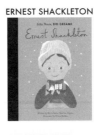

STEVE JOBS

AYRTON SENNA

LOUISE BOURGEOIS

ELTON JOHN

JOHN LENNON

PRINCE

CHARLES DARWIN

CAPTAIN TOM MOORE

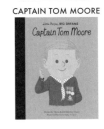

HANS CHRISTIAN ANDERSEN

STEVIE WONDER

MEGAN RAPINOE

MARY ANNING

MALALA YOUSAFZAI

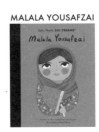

ANDY WARHOL

ACTIVITY BOOKS

STICKER ACTIVITY BOOK

COLORING BOOK

LITTLE ME, BIG DREAMS JOURNAL

Discover more about the series at www.littlepeoplebigdreams.com